ISBN – 9780998396712

Cover Design: Catherine Villeminot

Illustration: Jocelyn Haybittel Gibson

To order additional copies, please contact:

www.sarahcolton.com/bad-girls-perfume/

or

sarahcolton@me.com

❖Bad Girls Perfume NOTES❖

Sarah Colton

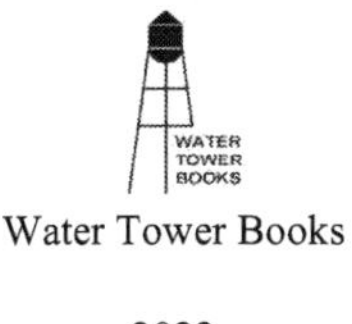

Water Tower Books

2022

"Finding a fragrance can be like finding a soul-mate."

- Sarah Colton

❖Contents❖

❖Intro❖

As an American perfume writer, journalist, and videographer living in Paris, I've spent a lot of time sniffing fragrances, especially during and since writing my book *Bad Girls Perfume Tips and Tales.* After years of chasing around after tiny pieces of paper, or notes written on perfume blotters, I realized that what I needed was a dedicated little perfume sniffing notebook small enough to carry around in my pocket or handbag, complete with bits of fragrance-specific info I can't always keep in my head. When some of my *perfumista* friends told me that's exactly what *they* needed too, I thought, HECK, make a bunch, and spread the wealth!

So here it is...*Bad Girls Perfume NOTES.*

In it you will find:
*Useful tips and questions to help you establish and appreciate your OWN personal relationship with fragrances.

*Thirty-eight pages for taking notes -- recording factual information about specific fragrances, as well as personal feelings, such as, impressions, likes, dislikes, moods, etc., PLUS inspirational quotes from *Bad Girls Perfume Tips and Tales* - just to keep your juices flowing.

*A handy-dandy Mini Lexicon of basic info about perfume ingredients, structure, classification methods, and commonly used terms to have at your fingertips just in case you can't remember them all.

And that's it. *Bad Girls Perfume NOTES.*

Enjoy. Happy Sniffing, and Stay BAD !

xxx Sarah and the Bad Girls at *Bad Girls Perfume*

❖Your Unique Relationship with Perfume❖

*What do you remember about your first perfume experience?

*How old were you?

*What were the circumstances?

*Was it associated with your mother, you father, a sibling, another significant person in your life, a stranger, a place, a mood?

*How did it make you feel?

*What do you associate with other memorable perfume experiences?

Can you think of another person in the world who would answer these questions exactly as you have done?

That's what I thought!

Your relationship with perfumes in general, or with a specific perfume, is UNIQUE.

Perfumes are highly evocative works of art that stir imagination through olfaction (smell), memory, and dreams.

The way a perfume smells to you is based on a singular combination of *facts*, such as the specific ingredients in its formula, and the unique make-up of your nasal and brain receptors, in combination with *feelings* it triggers, based on your memories, moods, and dreams.

So, never let anyone tell you you're wrong about the way a fragrance smells to you.

Transformational

If you're like me, you're probably always on the look-out, even at the unconscious level, for that *amazing* fragrance. The one that calls your name. The one that grabs you like a lover, takes you somewhere magic, and tells you something so profoundly personal that it literally *transforms* your life.

"Something in the way [Guerlain's] JICKY spoke to me on a profoundly deep level... not with words but with the unique power of her fragrance.... I felt her looking straight into places of my soul even I couldn't see....She saw who I was. She got who I was. And in this instant, my life was transformed. By a perfume." Bad Girls Perfume Tips and Tales, p.9-10.

I've only been transformed by a fragrance twice in my life, and I've sniffed *a lot* of fragrances. Each time I *knew*, and each time I bought it on the spot, knowing I would rather die or starve for the rest of my life than leave the store without it. And I've never regretted it.

When you find a *transformational* perfume, it's a rare moment you'll never forget. No use trying to explain it. Just, whatever you do, DON'T LET THIS ONE GO!

Besides this single piece of advice, you won't need anything else in this notebook – at least for a while. Because, when you find a *transformational* fragrance, and I hope you do, you'll have each other, the two of you will disappear into your private wonderland, and you won't give a damn about what I, or anyone, says about your choice, life in general, or anything, for that matter. Ahhh, the power of perfume!

I know, I know. I always tell people to be careful when they're sniffing. That fragrances evolve; that a fragrance you LIKE or even love on first whiff, might repel you later in its development, and that it's better to wait, get a sample if you can, spend 24 hours with it, etc. etc.. This is absolutely true for *most* fragrances, even the ones you like a lot. So, for *most* of time, here are my thoughts regarding your feelings about specific perfumes -- LIKE, DISLIKE and INDIFFERENCE.

<u>Indifference</u>

The worst feeling you can have about a fragrance, at least in my book, is INDIFFERENCE. Oh my god, get me away from here! Fragrances are about sensations and feelings, so if you feel indifferent to a perfume, move on. Maybe it smells like a thousand fragrances you've already smelled, or maybe it's just not your thing. What*ever*. Life's too short to waste another instant on it. Believe me, this simple action will save you a bunch of time by eliminating a HUGE number fragrances. Maybe 90%. YIKES. Don't quote me on this!

Like

Moving on to the good stuff, start by picking a perfume you LIKE, and apply it on your skin. No lightning bolts? *Pas de problème*. Perfumes can do lots of good things for us without having to transform our entire lives, such as supporting and comforting us by summoning important moods or qualities we might need for a specific day, situation, or moment. So, quieten your spirit and listen to what this one is saying to you. Is it yelling or whispering? Does it make you feel safe, powerful, or daring? Is it taking you to a place or a season? Is it channeling a significant person in your life, past or present? Is its message modern? Vintage? Sexy? Edgy? Mysterious, or exotic? Fresh, or dirty? Still interested? See if you can get a sample, take it home, wear it in several different contexts, take it to bed with you, and see how you feel about each other the next morning. Has it evolved into a 'lover' fragrance, or a new best friend? Then, maybe it's time to add it to your perfume collection, which you've surely realized by now, is nothing less than your own private support system. Or, GROSS get this stuff off me! Sad but true, there are plenty of fragrances I've loved on first sniff, and later (sometimes the next morning) can't stand. FYI these fragrances are referred to as 'scrubbers' among *perfumistas* because you really have to *scrub* to make them go away!

Hate

Oh yes, and what about fragrances you HATE on first whiff ? HATE is a powerful emotion. It's active, and like a perfume, can evolve in surprising ways. For this reason, it can be worth exploring fragrances you hate on a blotter even if you think you never want to put them on your skin. Lean in for a closer inspection. Is the repugnance you feel absolute and permanent, or does it evolve over time? Does it seem better or worse after half an hour, two hours, twenty-four? What is it that makes you hate it? Is it a fragrance, which though pleasing to others, elicits an emotional repugnance unique to you? Perhaps you associate it with a perfume worn by someone who's caused harm to you, or to someone you love. Or, is it triggering some kind of primal response of fight or flight, such as the smell of something dangerous to your health, like burning rubber or gasoline, or something sickening like rotting meat or excrement? Bear in mind that a perfume, like a painting or a musical composition, is a works of art, and repulsion *might* have been the *intention* of the artist (perfumer/nose), in which case, how well did they succeed?

Finally, does the fragrance evoke something about life in general, or perhaps even yourself, that you HATE? Is it something you truly hate, or could it be something you know is true, and have never wanted to admit? Ouch! And, WATCH OUT !! Like Petruchio and Katherina in Shakespeare's *The Taming of the Shrew*, some of the hottest, steamiest, and most ardent lovers in art, literature, and the world, HATED each other on first sight!

Whether you love or hate a perfume, allow your passions to run free when you're sniffing. Take risks. And TAKE NOTES!! Claim the pages in this notebook as *your* territory. Don't hold back. Go there. BE there. Spend as much time as you want. As much time as it takes. Trust me, when you find a truly *transformative* fragrance, you'll know! And even when you don't, your life will be richer for your forays and adventures into the deeply personal world to which only perfumes hold the key.

❖Perfume Notes and Inspirational Quotes❖

Facts and Feelings

FRAGRANCE FACTS

Name of fragrance:
Brand:
Creation Date:
Perfumer (Nose):
Family:

Structure:
Top Notes:

Heart Notes:

Bottom Notes:

FRAGRANCE FEELINGS

Transformational – Like – Dislike – Indifferent

WHY?

Impressions – Associations – Mood

"...Perfume is secret code for power....Perfume powers seduction. Perfume powers desire. Perfume powers a lot of life's experiences because it transforms feelings and perceptions.
Bad Girls Perfume Tips and Tales, p. 3-4.

FRAGRANCE FACTS

Name of fragrance:
Brand:
Creation Date:
Perfumer (Nose):
Family:

Structure:

Top Notes:

Heart Notes:

Bottom Notes:

FRAGRANCE FEELINGS

Transformational – Like – Dislike – Indifferent

WHY?

Impressions – Associations – Mood

"Bad Girls have been using perfume's vast powers to accomplish our objectives since the beginning of time.... Perfume is central to our illustrious Bad Girls birthright. This is simply who we are and how we operate."
Bad Girls Perfume Tips and Tales, p.12.

FRAGRANCE FACTS

Name of fragrance:
Brand:
Creation Date:
Perfumer (Nose):
Family:

Structure:

Top Notes:

Heart Notes:

Bottom Notes:

FRAGRANCE FEELINGS

Transformational – Like – Dislike – Indifferent

WHY?

Impressions – Associations – Mood

"...the most important fact worth remembering about perfume is that [we Bad Girls] are the ones who invented the whole damn thing in the first place! Perfume is our story. Just as much a part of us as our DNA. Using perfume to carry out our Bad Girl objectives is as natural to us as any other Bad Girl things we do." Bad Girls Perfume Tips and Tales. p.11.

FRAGRANCE FACTS

Name of fragrance:
Brand:
Creation Date:
Perfumer (Nose):
Family:

Structure:

Top Notes:

Heart Notes:

Bottom Notes:

FRAGRANCE FEELINGS

Transformational – Like – Dislike – Indifferent

WHY?

Impressions – Associations – Mood

"...An ace Bad Girl knows that through the judicious use of a well-chosen perfume she can actually become whatever persona she selects for a given Bad Girl job. More than playing a part, she IS this persona, thanks to the transformational power of perfume...."
Bad Girls Perfume Tips and Tales, p.15.

FRAGRANCE FACTS

Name of fragrance:
Brand:
Creation Date:
Perfumer (Nose):
Family:

Structure:

Top Notes:

Heart Notes:

Bottom Notes:

FRAGRANCE FEELINGS

Transformational – Like – Dislike – Indifferent

WHY?

Impressions – Associations – Mood

"...For strategic purposes Bad Girls sometimes need to work covertly, and at other times it's best to work in the open.."
Bad Girls Perfume Tips and Tales, p.15.

FRAGRANCE FACTS

Name of fragrancc:
Brand:
Creation Date:
Perfumer (Nose):
Family:

Structure:
Top Notes:

Heart Notes:

Bottom Notes:

FRAGRANCE FEELINGS

Transformational – Like – Dislike – Indifferent

WHY?

Impressions – Associations – Mood

"Throughout history, savvy Bad Girls have unerringly called upon the powers of soft pastel floral fragrances (think roses, violets, irises, peonies, freesias, and mimosas) as the perfect accomplices for their undercover persona."
Bad Girls Perfume Tips and Tales, p.16.

FRAGRANCE FACTS

Name of fragrance:
Brand:
Creation Date:
Perfumer (Nose):
Family:

Structure:

Top Notes:

Heart Notes:

Bottom Notes:

FRAGRANCE FEELINGS

Transformational – Like – Dislike – Indifferent

WHY?

Impressions – Associations – Mood

"...Bad Girls who know how to use "Innocent Flower" fragrances can get away with murder. As the unsurpassed undercover liars of perfume, pastel floral fragrances should be basic equipment in any Bad Girl's fragrance arsenal."
Bad Girls Perfume Tips and Tales, p.21.

FRAGRANCE FACTS

Name of fragrance:
Brand:
Creation Date:
Perfumer (Nose):
Family:

Structure:

Top Notes:

Heart Notes:

Bottom Notes:

FRAGRANCE FEELINGS

Transformational – Like – Dislike – Indifferent

WHY?

Impressions – Associations – Mood

"...if you take a deep whiff (especially of those innocent looking white ones), you may be taken aback by a not-so-innocent smelling, manifestly animalic odor. Oooh yes! Pastel florals might be the champions for undercover work, but white florals crush it for "In Your Face" Bad Girl jobs."
Bad Girls Perfume Tips and Tales, p. 21.

FRAGRANCE FACTS

Name of fragrance:
Brand:
Creation Date:
Perfumer (Nose):
Family:

Structure:

Top Notes:

Heart Notes:

Bottom Notes:

FRAGRANCE FEELINGS

Transformational – Like – Dislike – Indifferent

WHY?

Impressions – Associations – Mood

"...Though often misunderstood, chypre fragrances speak to the very soul of Bad Girls – strong, complex, sensual, and unstintingly committed to their cause. Depending upon their makeup, chypres can work both "Undercover" and "In Your Face," and can include a variety of floral, fruity, woody, and leather notes. Perhaps most importantly, once a chypre fragrance has become your ally she will never let you down."
Bad Girls Perfume Tips and Tales, p.39.

FRAGRANCE FACTS

Name of fragrance:
Brand:
Creation Date:
Perfumer (Nose):
Family:

Structure:

Top Notes:

Heart Notes:

Bottom Notes:

FRAGRANCE FEELINGS

Transformational – Like – Dislike – Indifferent

WHY?

Impressions – Associations – Mood

"Bad Girls are first and foremost players. Props and disguises. Schemes Laying traps. Acting out. Creating drama. Manipulating. Spying. Heating emotions past the boiling point. Anger. What could be more motivating than a desire for revenge? And nothing could be a better partner in crime for revenge than perfume."
Bad Girls Perfume Tips and Tales, p.57.

FRAGRANCE FACTS

Name of fragrance:
Brand:
Creation Date:
Perfumer (Nose):
Family:

Structure:

Top Notes:

Heart Notes:

Bottom Notes:

FRAGRANCE FEELINGS

Transformational – Like – Dislike – Indifferent

WHY?

Impressions – Associations – Mood

"...Whether practicing grand larceny, revenge, or petty thievery, don't forget your perfume, and remember to share the inspiration of your stories and fragrances with your Bad Girl friends!"
Bad Girls Perfume Tips and Tales, p.68.

FRAGRANCE FACTS

Name of fragrance:
Brand:
Creation Date:
Perfumer (Nose):
Family:

Structure:

Top Notes:

Heart Notes:

Bottom Notes:

FRAGRANCE FEELINGS

Transformational – Like – Dislike – Indifferent

WHY?

Impressions – Associations – Mood

"Although there's no such thing as a "Perfume Hunting License," if you think of perfume as being (metaphorically) at least as powerful as a loaded gun, you can understand the importance of knowing how to use it correctly."
Bad Girls Perfume Tips and Tales, p.69.

FRAGRANCE FACTS

Name of fragrance:
Brand:
Creation Date:
Perfumer (Nose):
Family:

Structure:
Top Notes:

Heart Notes:

Bottom Notes:

FRAGRANCE FEELINGS

Transformational – Like – Dislike – Indifferent

WHY?

Impressions – Associations – Mood

"...much has been written about the songs of Mermaids. Yet I'm here to tell you, Mermaids' real power is in their fragrance... [It] doesn't take much imagination to know they would smell like some combination of the tropical flowers they wear in their hair, the fruits and coconuts that grow on their islands, and the bracing ozone-y air of breaking waves..."
Bad Girls Perfume Tips and Tales, p.83.

FRAGRANCE FACTS

Name of fragrance:
Brand:
Creation Date:
Perfumer (Nose):
Family:

Structure:

Top Notes:

Heart Notes:

Bottom Notes:

FRAGRANCE FEELINGS

Transformational – Like – Dislike – Indifferent

WHY?

Impressions – Associations – Mood

"...[T]he most fascinating and alluring thing about a mermaid is the animalic, female odor of her tail. Without her tail, or the odor of her tail, a mermaid loses at least half her power."
Bad Girls Perfume Tips and Tales, p.83.

FRAGRANCE FACTS

Name of fragrance:
Brand:
Creation Date:
Perfumer (Nose):
Family:

Structure:
Top Notes:

Heart Notes:

Bottom Notes:

FRAGRANCE FEELINGS

Transformational – Like – Dislike – Indifferent

WHY?

Impressions – Associations – Mood

"...one of perfume's elemental strengths is its power to evoke the dark side. Whether truly The Dark Side, as in "Evil" with a capital E, or simply the incandescent feminine face of power, which has historically been associated with evil in all its forms. There can be no doubt that a cunning and crafty mix of perfumery and witchcraft is as good as bad gets!"
Bad Girls Perfume Tips and Tales, p.89.

FRAGRANCE FACTS

Name of fragrance:
Brand:
Creation Date:
Perfumer (Nose):
Family:

Structure:

Top Notes:

Heart Notes:

Bottom Notes:

FRAGRANCE FEELINGS

Transformational – Like – Dislike – Indifferent

WHY?

Impressions – Associations – Mood

"...Ultimately, all Bad Girls, whether they consider themselves to be witches or not, are born with an innate predisposition for the techniques of witchcraft. And savvy Bad Girls know you don't have to be a bonefide Witch with a capital 'W' (or 'B' as some like to think) to excel at this, as long as you use the most basic ingredient in all magic formulas: perfume.
Bad Girls Perfume Tips and Tales, p.96.

FRAGRANCE FACTS

Name of fragrance:
Brand:
Creation Date:
Perfumer (Nose):
Family:

Structure:
Top Notes:

Heart Notes:

Bottom Notes:

FRAGRANCE FEELINGS

Transformational – Like – Dislike – Indifferent

WHY?

Impressions – Associations – Mood

"Fantasies open a fabulous secret world to hide from or run to, alone, or in company. Who or what could be our best accomplice for such exploits? Perfumes, of course. As keepers of the gates to our wildest, deepest, and most intimate imaginations, perfumes can inspire, encourage, and accompany us through all our fantasies,...
Bad Girls Perfume Tips and Tales, p.99.

FRAGRANCE FACTS

Name of fragrance:
Brand:
Creation Date:
Perfumer (Nose):
Family:

Structure:
Top Notes:

Heart Notes:

Bottom Notes:

FRAGRANCE FEELINGS

Transformational – Like – Dislike – Indifferent

WHY?

Impressions – Associations – Mood

"...Chypre fragrances are warm, dry, animalic, and perilously sexy......"
Bad Girls Perfume Tips and Tales, p.39

FRAGRANCE FACTS

Name of fragrance:
Brand:
Creation Date:
Perfumer (Nose):
Family:

Structure:

Top Notes:

Heart Notes:

Bottom Notes:

FRAGRANCE FEELINGS

Transformational – Like – Dislike – Indifferent

WHY?

Impressions – Associations – Mood

"...although the best perfumes leave an indelible "trail," they will never betray our deepest secrets.... Unless, of course, we want them to."
Bad Girls Perfume Tips and Tales, p.99.

❖Mini-Lexicon❖

This Mini-Lexicon briefly defines and explains a few terms and expressions commonly used in perfumery. Obviously, there are many more that I won't include here, or we'll never get going. Should you have further questions, please feel free to contact me at www.badgirlsperfume.com and I'll be happy to answer them and/or refer you to one of my favorite Bad Girls Perfume Experts.

Table of Contents

Concentration Percentages of Fragrance Products

Most commercially available fragrances are composed of natural and synthetic fragrant oils in an alcohol and water base*.

Percentage of Fragrant Oils in Total Composition

- Pure Perfume, Perfume Extract (*extrait de parfum*), Perfume (parfum): 15-40% (average 25%)
- Eau de Parfum: 10-20% (average 15%)
- Eau de Toilette: 5-20% (average 10%)
- Eau de Cologne: 3-8% (average 5%)
- Cologne: up to than 4%
- Splashes less than 3%

*****

**The percentage of alcohol to water in the base can vary from 98% for perfume extracts to approximately 70% for colognes and splashes.*

The Perfume Pyramid

Classic perfume construction is a three-tiered organization of fragrant notes (individual natural or synthetic raw materials) often referred to as a pyramid, with top notes at the summit, heart notes in the middle, and base notes at the bottom.

Top Notes

Top Notes are the most volatile oils in a fragrance (they evaporate the most quickly) -- in the first few minutes of opening, and give the very first impression of the fragrance. Top notes are often citruses, light florals, or aromatic herbs (such as lavender and rosemary.

Heart Notes

Heart Notes make up the middle part of a fragrance formula. They are what you smell after the initial top notes have evaporated and before the base notes set in. Heart notes indicate the main traits of a fragrance's "personality." Heart notes typically contain floral, citrus, woody, green, or musky notes.

Base Notes

Base notes develop after the top and some of the heart notes have evaporated, are most evident in the latest stage of fragrance, and may stay for twelve hours or longer. Base notes are generally "heavy" such as woods, ambers, leathers, and musks.

Perfume Classification Systems

Although there are many classification systems, the two I use most are:

The SFP Classification System
Created by the Société Française de Parfumeurs, the SFP Classification System divides fragrances into seven olfactory "fragrance families": Citrus, Floral, Fougère (fern-like), Chypre, Woody, Amber, and Leather, each of which has sub-families such as "Woody Citrus", "Floral Fruity," etc.

Fragrances of the World® Fragrance Wheel Classification
Created by fragrance expert, Michael Edwards, the Fragrance Wheel, defines the relationship between four "Families" – Floral, Ambery, Woody, and Fresh – and illustrates how each evolves into fourteen fragrance sub-categories: Floral, Soft Floral, Floral Amber, Soft Amber, Amber, Woody Amber, Woods, Mossy Woods, Dry Woods, Aromatic, Citrus, Water, Green (smelling of cut grass or leaves), and Fruity.

The following section is an alphabetical list and brief description of the primary "Families" in both classifications. Of course, as we all know, perfume is an art form subject to individual interpretations (thank goodness!), which, like Bad Girls, can never be totally contained within anything so "rigid" as a classification. I like to think of perfume classifications as a conceptual "handle" by which to grasp a fragrance and hold it in my mind in relations to other fragrances.

Fragrance Families

Amber or Ambery - Typically smelling of resins, vanilla, incense, spices, and oud. Warm, sometimes very HOT, and sultry.

Aromatic - The name of this family can be confusing because in French 'aromatic' refers to any fragrant substance, while in English it often refers specifically to the sharp pungent fragrance of herbs such as lavender, sage, rosemary, etc..

Citrus – This family is characterized by the zesty smell of citrus fruits (orange, lemon, lime, neroli*, grapefruit, and bergamot**) which produce refreshing essences, and have been used in perfumery for millennia. Many perfumes and most colognes are part of the citrus family.
**Neroli is essential oil from BITTER orange trees;*
***Bergamot - a citrus fruit typically grown in Mediterranean regions that is slightly larger than a lemon and smaller than an orange. The distinctive smell of Earl Gray tea comes from bergamot.*

Chypre - A family of fragrances, usually built around a sharp contrast of citrus notes and a woody, oak-mossy accord, and named in honor of François Coty's 1917 fragrance, *Chypre*, one of the earliest fragrances bearing this accord. Coty named his fragrance after the island of Cyprus (Chypre in French), home for many aromatic shrubs, such as cistus labdanum, and famous throughout antiquity for the quality of its fragrances.

Floral –fragrances in this family replicate the scent of a single flower ("soli-flore") or a bouquet of flowers ("multi-flore").

Fougère – This family is characterized by a lavender, green, woody, and forest-y smell, and built on the blend of lavender, oak moss and coumarin. Named after the first fougère fragrance, Paul Parquet's 1882 Fougère Royale, and built on the imaginary scent of ferns (fougère means fern in French). Traditionally, masculine, and reminiscent of old-school shaving lotions and creams.

Gourmand – Though not considered a family or group in either the SFP, or the 'Fragrance Wheel' classifications, gourmand fragrances typically contain significant edible or food-smelling notes such as vanilla, candy, tonka beans, honey, chocolate, berries, cinnamon, cupcakes, whiskey, sugared almond, marzipan, and even cotton candy, or coffee. The French term "Gourmand" is often used to refer to a person with a sweet tooth.

Green- Fragrances of this group smell of cut grass or leaves. (Not considered a family in the SFP classification.).

Leather - dry, sometimes VERY dry notes, sometimes luxurious and sometimes rough, all meant to evoke the smell of leather or elements associated with leather tanning and preparation, such as smoke, burnt wood, honey, wood, wood tars, or tobacco.

Woody – Fragrances of the woody family smell warm and opulent like sandalwood and patchouli, or warm and dry like cedar, and vetiver.

Perfume Raw Materials

Plant Products

Amber - a general term referring to any number of fragrant blends made of resins such as, benzoin, galbanum and cistus labdanum. (See individual definitions of these resins below.)

Ambrette or Muskmallow –a type of hibiscus plant. Oil from its seeds has a musk-like odor and is frequently used to replace true musk.

Benzoin - an oil with a pleasantly antiseptic smell reminiscent of vanilla. In addition to its medicinal value as an antiseptic, benzoin is a common ingredient in incense and perfumes of the Amber family.

Cistus, Labdanum, Cistus Labdanum, or 'Rock Rose' - a resin or amber obtained from leaves and branches of a flowering shrub that grows in Mediterranean regions. With a sweet, woody, leathery smell often associates with churches or polished woods, Cistus Labdanum is part of the basic formula for chypre fragrances, and also common in amber and fougère fragrances.

Elemi- a gum resin with a light, fresh, balsamic-spicy, citrusy scent.

Galbanum - a plant resin with a bitter green smell, associated with amber fragrances.

Oak Moss - a tree material with a distinctive bitter, musty, smell, and an essential part of the distinctive scent of chypre fragrances.

Oud or Agarwood - an aromatic resinous substance that forms in evergreen aquilaria and gyrinops trees native to southeast Asia, when they have been infected with a certain type of fungus. Valued for its distinctive scent, characterized as soft fruity, floral, woody, or balsamic with shades of vanilla, musk, and ambergris.

Patchouli - a green busy herb that grows in India and Indonesia. The leaves are used in perfumery for their pungent sweet, dark, and earthy aroma.

Peti-Grain – the essential oil obtained from the leaves and twigs of the Bitter Orange tree (as opposed to Neroli which is oil obtained from Bitter orange FLOWERS).

Resin - a thick plant extract of similar consistency to molasses. Typical resins used in perfumery are cistus labdanum, benzoin, and galbanum.

Vetiver - a “beach grass” whose fragrant roots smell dry-edged, green, and earthy, recalling the mellow browns of cigars or of beautifully tanned leathers. There’s also a brightness to it, and a saltiness that makes me think of straw hats, beach mats, and sunshine. Traditionally used in men’s fragrances, vetiver has increasingly found its way into Bad Girls territory. Thank goodness. It’s one of my favorite raw materials!

Animal Products

Animal products were used in traditional perfumery for their erotic animalistic smells and also as fixatives for the other fragrant materials. Because of heightened concerns for animal rights among the general public, most fragrance materials derived from animal products are now banned, or have become so costly that they are seldom used in modern perfumery, and their odors have been replaced with synthetic molecules.

Ambergris - regurgitation (vomit) from sperm whales, which having floated and ripened for months or years on the sea, is washed up on shore. Ambergris is highly prized for its erotic odor and strong fixative qualities.

Castoreum - a leathery smelling secretion from the Castor beaver.

Civet - dander scraped from the hairs of Civet cats.

Hyraceum - fossilized badger urine with a complex smell similar to a combination of musk, castoreum, civet, tobacco, and oud (agarwood).

Musk - obtained by surgical removal from the "musk pod" (near sexual organs) of the Himalayan musk deer.

Synthetic Products

Chemical discoveries during the second half of the19th century had a game-changing impact on the world-wide perfume industry. Synthetic fragrance molecules offered scents otherwise unavailable, or difficult to obtain in nature, vastly increasing perfumers' fragrance palette and allowing them to create abstract fragrances beyond the natural realm. This can be compared to the availability of portable paint tubes for artists of approximately the same period, which allowed them to paint outside, instead of inside their studios. Both phenomena opened the way to enormous potential of "abstract", "impressionist" creations.

Indeed, it can be argued that thanks to the infinite possibilities synthetics bring to the perfumer's palette, fragrance making evolved from a "craft" to an "art" during this period, and led to the explosive growth and importance of the perfume industry at the beginning of the 20th century, and continues today.

In addition to being known for the variety and intensity of their smells, some synthetics (such as aldehydes), are appreciated in perfume compositions because of their capacity to enhance and boost (stir up) the diffusion of other raw materials in a formula, for a "shimmering" and "effervescent" delivery".

<u>Aldehydes</u> –chemical compounds, the best known of which are C10, C11, and C12, and made famous in CHANEL N°5.

<u>Ambroxan</u> - a synthetic compound created as a replacement for natural ambergris, used in may fragrances to create a voluptuous skin-like odor, and/ or to prolong the fragrance's *sillage.*

Calone - A synthetic raw material evoking the smell of fresh melon as well as the ethereal, ozon-y sensation of breaking waves, sea-breezes, and marine life. Calone is often used in marine or "aquatic" fragrances.

Coumarin – A synthetic fragrant molecule used in perfumery to add a sweet note suggestive of freshly mown hay or cut grass. In nature, coumarin is found in Tonka Beans, which grow on cumaru trees.

Ionone - a series of chemical substances used in many fragrances to create the smell of violets.

Vanillin – Smells like vanilla, and one of the most common synthetic perfume materials.

Natural Ingredients vs Synthetic Ingredients

Today, while the majority of fragrances are a mix of natural and synthetic ingredients, there are fragrances that are 100% natural, and others that are 100% synthetic. The choice is yours!

A Few Other Perfume Terms

Animalic - describes fragrances suggesting animal or bodily smells - sensual, musky, sweaty, etc..

Base – the primary (sometimes pre-composed) constituent of a fragrance's structure.

Perfume Notes - individual (natural or synthetic) raw materials, used in a fragrance composition.

Perfume Chords - several notes arranged to create a single harmonic or discordant effect.
Dissonance - inharmonious combination of notes or chords.

Sillage - This French term literally means the wake that a passing boat leaves in water. In perfumery it refers to the fragrance "trail" that lingers in the air or in memory after the wearer has gone.

Selective/Mass-tige Vs. Niche/Artisanal/ Fragrance Brands
Large brands (typically found in department stores, such as Chanel, Dior, Guerlain, YSL, etc.) are often referred to as "Selective" or "Mass-tige" brands, while smaller, less well-known "niche" brands, sometimes referred to as "artisanal", "creator", or "indie", are primarily sold in specialty perfume shops. As a general rule, "niche" brands are considered to be more 'confidential' because they do not advertise, and instead are discovered by word of mouth or through social media.

❖<u>Technical Support and Sources</u>❖

Société Française des Parfumeurs - Official Fragrance Catalogue and Terminology ®

Michael Edwards - <u>Fragrances of the World ® Fragrance Wheel Classification</u>

Bad Girls Perfume Tips and Tails, by Sarah Colton, Water Tower Books, 2016.

❖Parting Words❖

This should be enough to keep you going – at least for a while, my friend. So, I'm handing it over to you.

"It's your turn to write the next chapter in the fabulous history of Bad Girls Perfume, which as you undoubtedly know by now, is your own."
Bad Girls Perfume Tips and Tales. p.141.

xxx

Sarah Colton

and

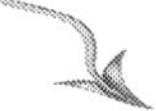

The Bad Girls at *Bad Girls Perfume.*

If you need help, give us a yelp at www.badgirlsperfume.com

❖About the Author❖

Sarah Colton is an American fragrance writer and videographer living in Paris, France. Her book, *Bad Girls Perfume Tips and Tales* published in 2016 won the prestigious Perfumed Plume Award® for best book in 2017, and has subsequently become a cult classic among *perfumistas* world-wide.

Made in the USA
Columbia, SC
08 June 2024